THE ALTRUISTS
BY NICKY SILVER

DRAMATISTS
PLAY SERVICE
INC.

The Altruists *is dedicated to Douglas Aibel,*
artistic director of my theatrical home.

THE ALTRUISTS received its world premiere at the Vineyard Theatre (Douglas Aibel, Artistic Director; Barbara Zinn Krieger, Executive Director; Jeffrey Solis, Managing Director) in New York City on February 20, 2000. It was directed by David Warren; the set design was by Neil Patel; the lighting design was by Kenneth Posner; the sound design was by John Gromada; the costume design was by Teresa Snider-Stein; and the production stage manager was Nancy Elizabeth Vest. The cast was as follows:

RONALD .... Joey Slotnick
SYDNEY .... Veanne Cox
LANCE .... Eddie Cahill
CYBIL .... Kali Rocha
ETHAN .... Sam Robards

CHARACTERS

RONALD, 29, a flamboyant dumpling.

SYDNEY, 34, high-strung, shallow and utterly self-absorbed.

LANCE, 20, not terribly bright but terribly sexy.

CYBIL, 28, the girl next door, beneath her tough veneer.

ETHAN, 32, sexy, manly and possibly British.

PLACE

New York City.

TIME

One Sunday.

THE ALTRUISTS

A light comes up on Ronald, who addresses the audience. He is in bed, but we cannot really see either his apartment or the person in bed next to him, who appears at the moment to be just a lump under the covers.

RONALD. I grew up in a beautiful house. Two parents, two children, three bedrooms. Two cars. A woman for cleaning. A man in the yard. A sky that was extremely blue, an azure blue, or cobalt. And I had no idea that the world was unfair. And when I saw, as I grew up, the world as it is, I dreamed that I could make a better place. Where people lived in rooms *not* doorways. Where children were cared for by parents until they no longer could, when, gladly and freely, the parents were cared for by children. And I had no idea what work, what draining work, what all-consuming, to the point that I have nothing, nothing in my life *but* work, kind of work it would be. I had no idea that making anything meant giving up everything. I had no idea apartments even came *as small as this*. But then, how could I? I grew up in a beautiful house with a swimming pool with a diving board and a changing room and fresh towels, put there by someone whom I never saw ... Good work, I found out, as I grew up, good work, my God, is just exhausting. *(The playing area is divided into three apartments. The light comes up on Sydney's, clearly once the nicest, now stripped of all its grandeur. There are discarded clothes hanging on a hall rack. Sydney, dressed chicly in a pink Richard Tyler suit, speaks to a lump in the bed, presumably Ethan.)*

SYDNEY. Ethan, I have had it! I can take it no more. Do you hear me? You can pretend to be asleep, I don't care. Pretend you don't hear me. Your whole life is nothing but pretense anyway! All your causes! Your walkathons and demonstrations! Your rallies and protests! Your firebombs and letter-writing! — I AM NOT HAPPY! How could I be? Am I supposed to enjoy your condescension? Should I love your humiliating me in front of your friends? I hate your friends. Cretins. Blowhards and Cretins, all of them. With all of your political babble. You care more about your receding hairline than the plight of the disenfranchised! You're more concerned with your thickening waist than the homeless and the needy! You're nothing but a bunch of phonies! How do you think I feel when I'm introduced as "just" an actress? As if what I did for a living didn't bring joy into the world! As if what I *do* for a living didn't make this life more bearable for the very disenfranchised you pretend to care about! There is dignity, profound dignity in my life, in my work! But you choose to sneer at it. People LOVE SOAP OPERAS! I get mail by the bushel, letters by the trillion! I have fans! I have followers! All over this country people are worried about Montana Beach! Will she leave Brock for Brick? Will she kick her ugly habit? Will she find her mother, true love or the meaning of life!? People care about me! Who cares about you?! I ask you. Who cares about you! Not I! Not I, Ethan! And yet you refer to me, with your little band of pseudo-left wing hooligans as "just an actress," "just a soap opera actress." And this, this after I let you use my home for your meetings — meetings!? Drunken frat parties! Bacchanalian orgies of cheap wine and non-ideas, in MY home! That's right. My home, this is my home! This bed is mine. These walls are mine. These sheets are mine! Mine, mine, mine, mine, mine! Everything is mine! You are nothing but a crummy little parasite with empty ideas, sponging off my hard work — and then you make me feel small because once, ONCE I owned a fur coat — IT WAS MY MOTHER'S! Well, I could survive that. I turned the other cheek, because I loved you — or I thought I did. I see now that I was just drunk with sex. That's what you do, you inebriate people with sex. So I could overlook your shabby treatment — because you have beautiful eyes and the stamina of a ten-year-old. Fine. Fine. Fine. And I can overlook the theft. The endless theft of my things by your merry band of so-called radicals. This was a lovely home! I had a lovely home! There was an ashtray from Paris. Gone. Stolen by that Gustavo who smells like a South American sheep farm. Vanished! There was my collection of first editions, one by one walked out the door. There was a Louis IVX armoire right here! And a Regency table! And matching nightstands! ALL GONE! I know what you're thinking. Those are just *things*. She's obsessed with *things*. Things own her. She loves her *things* more than she loves herself. Fine they were things … But they were MY THINGS! Besides, maybe you're right, maybe they are "just" things. Maybe I don't need them anymore. But the beauty part is — are you listening to me? — the beauty part is, I can buy *more* things! I can buy things over and over! I can buy things in duplicate and triplicate and whatever itricate means four, because I work! Because I have a job! So I let the things go. I wave good-bye, quietly, as my things walk out of the house in strange pockets and on rented hand trucks. "Good-bye things." Who needs them? And who needs you, Ethan? I say, not I! I am bigger than that. I let it go. I breathe and let the tragedy fall away from me like a cheap dress. And the drinking! I say, "He's human." The constant drinking, the stealing money from my purse for the constant drinking, night after night, week after week. The smell of sweat and whiskey on every Ralph Lauren sheet I own — I don't think that's the odor Ralph Lauren had in mind when he went into the home furnishings business!! I DON'T THINK SO! And the waiting, the hours stretched in front of me as I binge and purge and binge and purge and binge and purge waiting for a call, a word, a sign that you're alive, that you're drunk and staggering, but out there, somewhere alive! I learned to cope. I learned to cope when the call came from another woman's bed! "He has failings. I'm not giving. She was groping." Oh, the lies I've told myself. The endless song of lies and consolations. "It's not his fault," I told myself when you called from Monica Jeffrey's house purring apologies in a postcoital dream state. IT IS NOT APPROPRIATE TO APOLOGIZE FOR INFIDELITY WHILE STILL IN BED WITH THE OTHER WOMAN! Have you learned nothing in your thirty-one years on this planet? But I blamed her. "She was jealous, she was greedy and rapacious. She was wanton

and desperate! You were confused and disoriented. She had new breasts! I need new breasts!" Oh, the demented, self-flagellating diatribe I've heard in my head. But I survived! And I survived the call from Cynthia Brodrick's bed and Allison Seaver's. I survived the mocking, the ridicule heaped on every dress, blouse, skirt and suit I own! This is a Richard Tyler, Ethan! RICHARD TYLER! This suit costs enough to put one of your homeless children through medical school — but you laugh at it and point your finger because it's not ripped jeans with red wine stains, because it's not a torn T-shirt, shrunk down and stretched out, emblazoned with some idiotic political slogan or symbol! BECAUSE IT'S NOT BLACK! You sneer at Chanel and Gucci and Azadine Alaia because nothing they make reads "Gay Power" or "Black Power" or "Fur Is Killing" across the tits! Fine! Make fun of me! Fine! Torment me! I can take it! Just as I can take the vicious things you said to my mother, granted, a miserable woman, but she never did you any harm! NOT ONE BIT OF HARM! And yet you thought it amusing to tell her on the phone that'd I'd been killed, stabbed to death by my lesbian lover! YOU ARE EVIL ITSELF! EVIL DISGUISED AS ALTRUISM! I see that now! Then, oh then, I chalked it up to a wry sense of humor. You have no sense of humor! YOU ARE NOT FUNNY! AND ANOTHER THING — *(Her light goes out abruptly. Light comes up on Ronald's apartment. A dingy studio, full of junk. Ronald and Lance, wearing underwear are in bed. Ronald's T-shirt has a Black Power fist on it. Lance is air-drumming frenetically. Ronald lights a cigarette.)*
RONALD. That was great.
LANCE. You were great.
RONALD. *You* were great.
LANCE. No, man! Man! Listen to me, man! You were great. Fuckin' great.
RONALD. *(Coy.)* I don't know.
LANCE. No man! You were, man!
RONALD. Well, thanks. I —
LANCE. D'ya have any coke?
RONALD. What?
LANCE. D'ya have any coke?
RONALD. Look in the fridge.

LANCE. What?

RONALD. There's Diet Coke, I think. In the fridge.

LANCE. No, man. Coke. Like, coke. Y'know, coke. Coke ... Coke.

RONALD. ... No.

LANCE. Shit.

RONALD. Sorry. *(Lance drums away for a moment.)*

LANCE. Angel dust? *(Their light goes out. Sydney's light returns. She is as she was.)*

SYDNEY. Was I hurt when you threw my plants out the window!? I was. I cared for those plants! I loved them! I watered them and loved them since they were seeds! They were like my children! But they were, after all, just plants. And, as you pointed out, you didn't hit anyone, you didn't kill anyone when you hurled the pots, the terra-cotta pots from the fifteenth floor! And you were drunk or high on some substance, purchased, no doubt with money taken from MY purse! So I released. I HAVE BEEN HEROIC! Only a heroine, only a mythic figure, could overcome the scolds and the scandals — when you told everyone we knew, my friends, my family, MY THERAPIST, whom you had no business talking to in the first place — when you told everyone in New York City that I gave you syphilis, when we both know, we know without a doubt that Maria Portnoy gave you syphilis during that demonstration — and you in turn gave it to me! THAT WAS NOT FUNNY! I made allowances because every now and then, once a week, once a month, once in a blue moon, you made love to me and I saw fireworks, I heard orchestras! You made love to me and I remembered the beginning, when we made love nonstop, like Olympians! I put up with everything, I entered your world of East Village, Alphabet City, anti-trend-trendies, of sit-ins and marches and protests, because it felt good to have you inside of me! But no more! NO MORE, ETHAN! I'M A PERSON! I HAVE FEELINGS! I HAVE A BREAKING POINT AND I HAVE REACHED IT! Maybe I expect too much. Maybe I do. Maybe I'm looking for perfection. No man's perfect — BUT SOME ARE BETTER! And I have had it! LAST NIGHT WAS IT! When you refused to hold me, when you muttered some other name in your sleep, when you tried to kill me, when you held a pillow over my

11

face, in an ugly, violent attempt to snuff out my life, I REALIZED ... THINGS ARE NOT GOING WELL! *(Sydney's light goes out. Light comes up on Ronald and Lance, who continues "drumming.")*

RONALD. You know, I want you to know, I think you're very special.

LANCE. I think you're special too, man.

RONALD. No I mean it.

LANCE. I mean it too, man.

RONALD. Excuse me, but do you end every sentence with the word "man"?

LANCE. What?

RONALD. Good.

LANCE. You got any hash, man?

RONALD. Damn.

LANCE. What?

RONALD. No.

LANCE. Shit.

RONALD. I was saying, you are really very special. I've never experienced lovemaking like that before. I don't know if I can express my feelings. i'm a social worker, not a poet. I deal with the downtrodden, not with words. But making love to you was amazing. You really are an athlete. And, my God, so beautiful.

LANCE. You got any *booze?*

RONALD. *(Thinks for a moment.)* There might be something left over from a Seder. — No, we used that on ice cream. *(Their light goes out. Sydney's returns. She is now a crumbled weeping mess.)*

SYDNEY. I hope you're not hurt. I hope I haven't wounded you. I mean that. Because you are a light that shines in my life. You are a beam, Ethan, that illuminates every corner of my life. You're so good. You're a martyr. You're a saint, devoting your life to other people. I'm nothing! I'd be lost without you. I'd be desperate. I'm greedy and empty and foul. I know that. I do. But, still, it's true, as I was regaining consciousness this morning, I knew things had to change. As I traced through the events of our cohabitation, I realized I can't go on any longer, watching everything I own, everything I *am* walk away from me! It's over! It's all over! *I* must walk away! — I mean emotionally, you understand, this is my home — I must free myself!! ... Well? ... Have you nothing to say to me?

12

Don't you care if I throw away everything we've had? Ethan? Are you really so indifferent to us, the being of us, that you won't lift a finger, say a word to salvage it? ... *(Gaining strength.)* You are just hateful!! You are just a destructive power in a pretty package! That's what you are! I realized that as I gasped for breath under the weight of my pillow, pushed over my face by your beautiful hands. I saw, in a flash, that you're like a poison, seeping, seeping into every room of me! I HATE YOUR GUTS! ... Stop me, please! I LOVE YOU! ... No, no. Strength, strength, I will have strength! I will have courage! You've made me an addict! I've lost everything. My home is bare but for some old shoes and a *jockstrap* hanging over the shower! I have to free myself of you! You! You, who fills me with guilt because I eat meat, because I eat grapes, pay a woman to clean, drive a new car, belong to a union, ONCE WORE A FUR, WEAR LIPSTICK AND MAKEUP WITH-OUT EVER KNOWING *WHAT THE FUCK IT WAS TESTED ON,* BECAUSE I LIKE TIMES SQUARE BETTER, *BETTER* BECAUSE I FEEL SAFER, NOW THAT THE PIMPS AND THE WHORES AND HOMELESS ARE HERDED AWAY!! I WILL! ETHAN! I WILL FREE MYSELF OF YOU!! *(She produces a gun from her purse.)* Stop me. One word. One gesture! The smallest movement and I'll melt into your arms! I'll forgive you! I swear! We can go back to what we hoped our relationship would be, before it turned out to be what it is! TELL ME YOU LOVE ME!!! *(There is a long pause. Getting no response, she shoots the gun three times at "Ethan," then lets it drop to the floor.)* Shit. *(After a moment of horror, she flees the scene, pausing to adjust her hair in the hall rack mirror. Sydney's light goes out. The light on Ronald and Lance returns. Lance is still "drumming.")*
RONALD. I was saying, Lance ...
LANCE. Yeah?
RONALD. Don't do that — *(Lance stops drumming.)* You are really a gift. A very wonderful gift-like thing. I don't know what cosmic force drew me to that bar last night. I'd never been in that bar. I don't go to bars. I don't go out. I don't leave the house. I don't leave the room. Socially, really. But last night, there was a flood — the toilet backed up because the people upstairs flushed a sweatshirt down theirs. The toilet backed up and I went out. I had to go, you know

what I mean? I didn't even know that was a gay bar. I had no idea.
I suppose the name might've tipped some people off, Ramrod, but
I had no idea. And when I looked across the room and saw you
there, sitting at the bar, drumming away, like a frenzied, hopped-up
maniac, I knew that kismet drew me there, kismet drew me to that
bar, and into your eyes and your arms — and your heart, I hope.

LANCE. *(Drumming again.)* Sure.

RONALD. Because you're in my heart. I hope you believe me. I
haven't loved anyone in a very long time. I haven't been with anyone, it seems, since the continents were connected. I haven't given
my heart to a living soul. You're beautiful. What do you weigh? Do
you know?

LANCE. Beats me.

RONALD. It doesn't matter. You're perfect. You have the most
beautiful eyes. Did I mention that? What is that color? What do
you call that color?

LANCE. Blue.

RONALD. "Blue." "Blue." It's poetry. It's a song. And when I
looked into them, from across the sea of disaffected poseurs —

LANCE. What?

RONALD. Gay men.

LANCE. Oh.

RONALD. When our eyes met, I knew that my life was at a fork
in the road. I knew that something bigger than you and I and God
was at play. And then last night when we made love, I found out
that I was right. What I'm trying to say —

LANCE. *(Stops drumming.)* Yeah, fuck man, what are you saying?

RONALD. What I'm trying to say is, I know it's irrational, but I
have feelings for you. Real feelings. Not imagined feelings. I mean,
I know it's fast, but is there really a time table for this sort of thing?
What I'm telling you is, I believe, don't laugh, I believe that I am
in love with you. I believe ... that I have fallen in love with you.

LANCE. ... Wow.

RONALD. It's true.

LANCE. No shit?

RONALD. No.

LANCE. Cool.

RONALD. I want to stay in bed with you forever. I want to grow

14

old in this bed, on these sheets, in these underpants.
LANCE. Well —
RONALD. Damn. What time is it?
LANCE. I dunno.
RONALD. It must be noon. I have to go — I know! Come with me! Stay with me. Spend the day with me!
LANCE. What?
RONALD. I have to get to the park. They'll be waiting.
LANCE. Who?
RONALD. We're going to band together and fight for what's ours. The underclass rising up, flexing their muscles. The world is full of hatred and violence! And it's our job, Lance, our duty to stomp the living daylights out of it! Be part of that. Come with me, Lance.
LANCE. Well, I could but ...
RONALD. What?
LANCE. You hafta pay me for last night first.
RONALD. Pardon? *(Their light goes out. A light comes up on Cybil's apartment, a studio, messy and decrepit, filled with filthy junk — there is one beautiful piece of furniture: a Regency nightstand, very much out of place. Cybil is standing, talking to a lump in the bed, Ethan. She is wearing black jeans, cut off at knicker-length, and T-shirt reading "We're Here! We're Queer! Get Used to It." She is nearly always strident.)*
CYBIL. Get up! *(Ethan rolls over and moans.)* Get up, get up, get up, get, up! *(He emerges, groggy, from under the comforter.)*
ETHAN. What time is it?
CYBIL. I don't know, noon.
ETHAN. I want to sleep.
CYBIL. Ten. Two. Four. I don't know what time it is.
ETHAN. Let me sleep.
CYBIL. We have to get to the park. What's wrong with you? They're counting on me. I'm bringing firebombs.
ETHAN. Huh?
CYBIL. They're waiting for us. — firebombs? Did I say firebombs? Is today firebombs or stink bombs? What's today?
ETHAN. Sunday.
CYBIL. *(Definite now.)* Stink bombs. Firebombs — it doesn't

matter. Get up!

ETHAN. Talk lower.

CYBIL. Get up, get up, get up, get up!

ETHAN. Ten more minutes.

CYBIL. You can't stay here, you can't be here! What if Audrey walks in?!

ETHAN. *(Lewd.)* What if she does, Cookie?

CYBIL. Don't call me Cookie.

ETHAN. What if she does?

CYBIL. What if she does? She'd kill you. I mean that literally. She would get your head in a half nelson and snap your neck like a chicken. — Do these pants look OK?

ETHAN. She'd snap my neck?

CYBIL. She can bench-press 270 — jerk 350. Audrey is not to be fucked with. She has rages. She has tempers. She has a record.

ETHAN. My head hurts.

CYBIL. From what? I was there. What'd you do? Smoke some pot, drink three, four, five bottles of wine? Jesus Christ, MEN ARE SUCH WEAKLINGS!

ETHAN. My head is falling apart. Pieces of my head are all over the floor.

CYBIL. Do these pants look all right!?

ETHAN. They look fine.

CYBIL. They were full-length last week.

ETHAN. Oh?

CYBIL. The rats ate 'em to knickers. *(Their light goes out. Ronald's light returns. He and Lance are as they were.)*

RONALD. Pay you?

LANCE. Yeah.

RONALD. Pay you?

LANCE. Yeah.

RONALD. Pay you?

LANCE. Yeah. *(Their light goes out. Cybil's returns. She and Ethan are as they were.)*

ETHAN. Please stop shouting.

CYBIL. I didn't say anything.

ETHAN. Oh dear God.

CYBIL. But you have to leave! We're supposed to assemble at one, or two or three-thirty.

ETHAN. For what?

CYBIL. What?

ETHAN. Assemble for what?

CYBIL. The rally!

ETHAN. What rally?

CYBIL. Tompkin's Square. It's Sunday, isn't it. You said it was Sunday.

ETHAN. Oh, the rally.

CYBIL. It's important! People are counting on us. Gustavo's bringing placards, I'm bringing firebombs. Or stink bombs, whatever. Both.

ETHAN. All right, all right.

CYBIL. I wish I could remember.

ETHAN. Remind me.

CYBIL. What?

ETHAN. What's it for?

CYBIL. What?

ETHAN. The rally? What's it for? *(They look at each other for a very long moment.)*

CYBIL. *(Annoyed.)* It'll come to me! *(Their light goes out. Ronald's returns.)*

RONALD. Pay you?

LANCE. What'd you think?

RONALD. I thought we met. I thought we did the dance that lovers do. I thought you liked me. I thought you cared for me. I care for you, don't you care for me? Tell me. Be honest. I can take it. Don't spare my feelings.

LANCE. Well —

RONALD. Tell me you love me! Don't tell me I'm nothing to you! I'll die! Do you hear me!? What do I have? I'm so goddamn lonely! I sit in a cubicle all day long, filling out forms, staring at corkboard. Devoting one's life to others is so depressing! Please tell me that I'm special to you!

LANCE. Sure, man. You're special.

RONALD. Thank God! Thank God you said that! You could have killed me. A cold word from you would kill me! A cutting remark would be a bullet in my head!

LANCE. Don't freak out.

RONALD. *(Thrilled.)* You care about me!

LANCE. Sure, fine. Whatever.

RONALD. *(More so.)* And you're a prostitute!

LANCE. Yeah, so?

RONALD. A wayward child. A lost soul, a dead leaf floating downstream! You've been sent to me, it's obvious. Fate brought you to my arms so that I could help you, rescue you. You are my vocation made real! Let me help you. Tell me your story.

LANCE. Well, I was born in Montana, but my mother —

RONALD. This is so exciting! I love a project! I love your hair and your eyes and your sweaty-tasting skin — I'll pull you into life, without the bureaucratic red tape. Stay with me!

LANCE. Well, I should call Scar ...

RONALD. Scar?

LANCE. My pimp.

RONALD. I see. *(Their light goes out. Cybil's returns. Ethan is putting on a T-shirt that reads "FUCK _____" [insert the name of the present mayor of New York].)*

CYBIL. Hurry up, hurry up, hurry up, hurry up!

ETHAN. *(Flat, not moving.)* I'm hurrying.

CYBIL. You have no idea what Audrey's capable of. She's insane. We were in Tijuana last winter and she put out the eyes of a man who just looked at me!

ETHAN. Are you serious?

CYBIL. Both eyes! With darts. Her aim is uncanny!

ETHAN. He looked at you?

CYBIL. Well, during sex. We were having sex. The man and I, not Audrey and I.

ETHAN. You're a very bad lesbian.

CYBIL. I can't remember his name. I think it started with an L. Lawrence? Larry? Lester? Shit.

ETHAN. She put out his eyes with darts?

CYBIL. We were in a bar.

ETHAN. Did she throw them one at a time, or both at once?

CYBIL. Leonard? Leland? What was it? Shit. This is gonna drive me crazy! *(Their light goes out. Ronald's returns. He and Lance are as they were.)*

RONALD. And he beats you?

LANCE. I deserve it.

RONALD. No one deserves to be beaten!

LANCE. I do. I steal from him sometimes. And I put shit in his blow.

RONALD. Oh you poor desolate lamb! You need me! I need you! I need contact, human contact. Social services is just paper pushing and phone interviews. *"How* many more children Miss Juarez? And the father is *where?"* We'll have a brilliant life together! Let me show you the city.

LANCE. I live on the streets.

RONALD. I'll show you the *in*doors!

LANCE. You gotta pay.

RONALD. *(After a moment of internal debate.)* All right. I'm not offended. I understand. Your identity, your self worth, it's all dependent on the exchange of funds. That's all you've ever known. I understand you, Lance. I love you. How much?

LANCE. Well, three hundred dollars for last night —

RONALD. Fine.

LANCE. And three hundred more for the hour.

RONALD. Fine.

LANCE. If you want me to stay.

RONALD. I do.

LANCE. Cool. *(Ronald goes through his wallet.)*

RONALD. Take a check?

LANCE. You got ID? *(Their light goes out. The light comes up on Sydney's apartment for a moment. There is no activity. The lump is still there. That light goes out. The light comes up on Cybil's apartment. Ethan is looking for his pants.)*

CYBIL. Leander? Lionel? Shit, shit, shit.

ETHAN. Let it go.

CYBIL. That's not it. *(He finds a take-out cup of coffee on the floor.)*

ETHAN. No. I mean, let it go. — When's this from?

CYBIL. It was here when I moved in.

ETHAN. When was that?

CYBIL. Three years ago. *(He downs the coffee.)* Hurry up!

ETHAN *(Tossing the cup.)* I feel like me again!

CYBIL. The crowd will be forming. The throng'll be ready to lift

19

its voice in defiance! FUCK THE PIGS!

ETHAN. What's it for? *(He finds his pants, black jeans, of course, and puts them on.)*

CYBIL. ... Squatters! That's it! We're supporting squatters! They're arresting squatters! The pigs! The fascist Nazi bullies! Rounding 'em up! Throwing them out! They have a right to live! They need to sleep and eat and breathe! They're people! Hurry up! The squatters need us!! FUCK THE MAYOR! FUCK CITY HALL! FUCK THE COPS!! FUCK THE YUPPY SCUM WITH THEIR FRENCH RESTAURANTS AND REAL-ESTATE PRICES AND BABY GAP AND NINE-DOLLAR MOVIES AND STARBUCKS! FUCK CAPPUCCINO AND FRAPPUC-CINO AND MOCHACCINO! FUCK BANANA REPUBLIC AND POTTERY BARN!! FUCK J.CREW AND THE MULTI-PLEXES AND GENTRIFICATION AND WHO THE FUCK DO THEY THINK THEY ARE EXPLOITING THIRD-WORLD LABOR AT SLAVE WAGES TO WALK THEIR BABIES IN MULTIPLE-SEAT STROLLERS!!

ETHAN. Squatters was last week.

CYBIL. Really?

ETHAN. Yes.

CYBIL. Shit.

ETHAN. *(Putting on shoes, Doc Martens, of course.)* This is for?

CYBIL. *(Fist in air.)* FREE NELSON MANDELA!!

ETHAN. He's free.

CYBIL. What?

ETHAN. Nelson Mandela is free.

CYBIL. Since when?

ETHAN. Long time.

CYBIL. Jesus Christ! You turn your back for a minute, one fuck-ing minute and they free Nelson Mandela!

ETHAN. So today is ... ?

CYBIL. I can't remember!!

ETHAN. My feet hurt where you bit me.

CYBIL. MEN ARE SUCH BABIES!

ETHAN. I'm not walking. I'm not carrying all that shit. I'll carry fire bombs or stink bombs, but I refuse to carry both.

CYBIL. We'll take a cab. Do you have any money?

ETHAN. Do you?

CYBIL. Audrey doesn't let me. She says I can't be trusted. She says I lose it. She says I can't remember ... what was I saying?

ETHAN. You don't have any money?

CYBIL. No.

ETHAN. Let's drive.

CYBIL. You have a car?

ETHAN. We can use Sydney's. I'll pick it up, bring it back here and we'll load up the trunk.

CYBIL. By the time you walk to her house, we could walk to the rally!

ETHAN. With all that stuff?!

CYBIL. Fine. You go. I'll wait here in case Gustavo calls. *(Ethan walks, in obvious pain, toward the door.)*

ETHAN. You bite hard.

CYBIL. MEN ARE SUCH PUSSIES!! Weaklings! Oppressive, borderline-idiot-weakling-pussies! — Here. *(She hands him a can of red spray paint.)* In case you pass fur coats on the way.

ETHAN. Right.

CYBIL. Keep your eyes peeled for Joan Rivers! *(He exits. Their light goes out. Ronald's light returns. Ronald and Lance are putting on black jeans and Doc Martens.)*

RONALD. How long has Scar — that was his name, right?

LANCE. Yeah.

RONALD. How long has Scar exploited you?

LANCE. Exploited?

RONALD. And oppressed you with his economic shackles.

LANCE. Oh, we don't do that shit, man. We don't play that game. I mean once, we did too much junk and he tied me up, but just that once.

RONALD. Oh my God.

LANCE. It was cool.

RONALD. You poor, misguided angel!

LANCE. You ever get tied up?

RONALD. God no.

LANCE. It's cool.

RONALD. You love your captor! That's so sad. That's so typical. You have to leave him, Scar, I mean.

21

LANCE. I dunno, man. I owe him big time. He got me the fucking coolest knife for Christmas last year. It was black and there was a scull on the handle. And on my birthday, fantastic fuckin' crystal meth.

RONALD. That's sweet — but trust me. Your life is going to run out. Your youth'll go down the drain. Get away from him. Get away from him now!

LANCE. And go where, man?

RONALD. Here.

LANCE. What?

RONALD. Stay here.

LANCE. You'll be my pimp?

RONALD. That's not what —

LANCE. I don't work Mondays and holidays.

RONALD. No, no, no. All of that is behind you now. Live here. With me. I'll help you. I can. I'll see to it that you finish school — did you finish school?

LANCE. No.

RONALD. I'll see to it you do.

LANCE. School sucks.

RONALD. You say that now, but you'll see, it's your ticket to a future.

LANCE. They kicked my ass out for a knife fight in the gym.

RONALD. I'll take care of you and provide for you and nurture you. I'll see to it that you're safe and happy and that you find something, *something* to do with your life that fills you up in ways you can't imagine.

LANCE. You mean *live* here?

RONALD. Yes.

LANCE. You mean, like, I'd have my own address?

RONALD. Yes.

LANCE. And a shelf in the fridge?

RONALD. Yes.

LANCE. And a box under the bed where I could keep my crack?

RONALD. *(Less committed.)* All right.

LANCE. You're really cool, man.

RONALD. *(À la Lance.)* No. No, man! You're really cool.

LANCE. What if I get on your nerves?

RONALD. You won't.

LANCE. I might.

RONALD. I'll go for a walk.

LANCE. What if you get on my nerves?

RONALD. I'll change. *(Simple, real. He strokes his hair.)* Listen to me. Listen to me, Lance, I mean this. I want to be your lover. I want more than that. I want to be your brother and your helper. I know your life has been hard but it'll be easier now. There's two of us. I want you to feel safe here. This'll be our home — not mine, not yours. Ours. I was beginning to worry that I'd be alone forever. I'm so happy. I'm so profoundly happy, that I found you ... I love you.

LANCE. *(Simply.)* OK then. *(They kiss, sweetly. There's a knock at the door. Ronald opens it, revealing Sydney.)*

SYDNEY. Ronald!

RONALD. Sydney? *(The light in Ronald's apartment goes out. The light in Sydney's comes up. Ethan addresses the lump in the bed.)*

ETHAN. Sydney, I'm taking the car. *(The light in Sydney's apartment goes out. The light in Ronald's returns.)*

RONALD. Sydney! What are you —

SYDNEY. I have to talk you! You have to help me. Do you have a phony passport?

LANCE. I do.

SYDNEY. Who are you?

RONALD. Lance, this is my sister, Sydney. Sydney, this is Lance.

SYDNEY. Nice to meet you.

LANCE. You look familiar.

SYDNEY *(Coy.)* From Montana Beach.

LANCE. Montana's landlocked. I was born there.

SYDNEY. It's a name! It's my character's name! And the name of the show!

LANCE. Sorry.

SYDNEY. I am so tired of that question!

LANCE. I remember now. I seen that show. It's dope, man.

SYDNEY. Pardon me?

LANCE. It's dope.

SYDNEY. What?

LANCE. Dope.

SYDNEY. What?

LANCE. Dope.
SYDNEY. What?
RONALD. *(Translating.)* Good.
SYDNEY. Thanks.
LANCE. Gotta joint?
SYDNEY. Here. *(She hands him a joint from her purse.)*
LANCE. Thanks.
RONALD. What are you doing here? Are coming to the rally?
SYDNEY. God no. God forbid. Grass stains and sun damage and
people of indiscriminate gender smelling sweaty. — I need help!
I'm in trouble. I mean it. This is serious!
RONALD. What is it?
SYDNEY. Can I speak to you privately?
RONALD. Lance is my partner now. We share everything. I hide
nothing.
LANCE. *(Toking up.)* This is good shit, man.
SYDNEY. Hmmm.
LANCE. It's the bomb.
SYDNEY. What?
LANCE. The bomb.
SYDNEY. What?
LANCE. The bomb.
SYDNEY. What?
RONALD. *(Translating.)* Dope.
SYDNEY. Oh.
RONALD. We're life partners. I found him, lost and lonely, ran-
dom notes without order —
SYDNEY. *(Knowing full well.)* He's a whore?
RONALD. Was!
SYDNEY. Oh God, Ronald. Not again.
LANCE. Again?
SYDNEY. You always do this.
RONALD. I don't know what she's talking about. I don't know
what you're talking about. I've never paid for sex in my life. I've
never been with a pro.
SYDNEY. No. But you go overboard. You always go overboard. I
mean if you like a hustler, for God's sake, buy him a watch like
everyone else.

24

RONALD. I don't *like* him!
LANCE. What?
RONALD. I love him!
SYDNEY. Like you loved that third-world girl you got from TV?
LANCE. You got a girl from TV?
SYDNEY. Yes.
LANCE. Cool.
RONALD. I did not GET a girl! I sponsored a girl — a little Ethiopian girl. I was twelve. She was six. She was darling —
LANCE. Cool.
RONALD. You get a photo. Big brown eyes, sad enough to break your heart! She was pretty and little, with dirt smeared all over her face. And for less than the cost of a cup of coffee a day —
SYDNEY. He was twelve. He sent her every penny he had! He sent her his allowance — wasn't enough, so he got a job.
RONALD. Someone has to help those people. And I'm proud to have done it!
SYDNEY. He swept up hair in the barber shop, after school. He sent her that money! THAT wasn't enough, he got a second job! A third job! A fourth and a fifth job! Until he had to be hospitalized for exhaustion!
RONALD. It was mono!
SYDNEY. It was exhaustion! And then, there in the hospital you ran into other people who'd adopted children from TV — and you all compared pictures! Remember that?!
RONALD. No! No, I don't! I remember none of this!
SYDNEY. You all compared pictures, I remember! You all compared pictures and they were ALL THE SAME! YOU ALL ADOPTED THE SAME DAMN THIRD-WORLD CHILD!
RONALD. I choose to believe they were similar! Merely similar!
SYDNEY. They were the same! It's a racket!
LANCE. *(Amused.)* They fucked you, man!
SYDNEY. Somewhere in the third world is one fabulously wealthy little girl with big brown sad eyes!
RONALD. Have you burst into my home to merely ridicule me?
SYDNEY. God! I forgot! I've done a horrible thing! I'm serious. This is a matter of life or death!
RONALD. What happened?

SYDNEY. *(Lying.)* I feel faint. *(To Lance.)* Would you go to the corner and get me a banana. I'm hypoglycemic.

LANCE. Whatever.

RONALD. We have bananas.

SYDNEY. Did I say a banana? I meant a mango.

RONALD. We have mangos.

SYDNEY. Pineapple.

RONALD. Got 'em.

SYDNEY. Pears?

RONALD. Got 'em.

SYDNEY. Guava?! I need a guava!

RONALD. Fine. Fine. Fetch Her Highness a guava.

SYDNEY. I'm hypoglycemic.

LANCE. You said that.

RONALD. You are not.

LANCE. Whatever it means.

SYDNEY. *(To Ronald.)* You don't know! *(To Lance.)* Here. Here's twenty dollars. Be a cherub and get me a guava. *(Lance takes the money.)*

RONALD *(Stopping him.)* You will come back, won't you?

LANCE. Fuck you man! Fuck you! You tryin' to insult me!?

RONALD. No.

LANCE. You think I'd steal her fuckin' twenty bucks?!

RONALD. I'm sorry —

LANCE. I got morals! I mean I'd fuck her up the ass for a hundred but I wouldn't rip her off. *(Lance exits.)*

RONALD. I'm dizzy with new love!

SYDNEY. *(Satisfied.)* Well, you've seen the last of him.

RONALD. You are so cynical. Lance is a darling boy! A sad fallen angel.

SYDNEY. Please. He doesn't even speak English.

RONALD. Language is a mutable, ever-evolving thing!

SYDNEY. You're paying him aren't you?

RONALD. Why can't you ever support me? You've never liked anyone I loved!

SYDNEY. Because I'm sane. Because I have standards. Because you become infatuated, over and over, with the lowest form of scum alive.

RONALD. Scum?!

SYDNEY. Murderers and convicts, drug addicts and prostitutes!

RONALD. They are people just like you and I — you're no one to judge. I know all about you. I know you better than you think. I know you take pills to sleep and pills to diet and pills to wake up —

SYDNEY. Those are prescription!

RONALD. Pills to calm down —

SYDNEY. MOST of those are prescription!

RONALD. How dare you come in here — aren't I entitled to some happiness. Lance means everything to me! You have no right to burst into my home and make judgments! Get out!

SYDNEY. Fine! Fine! I care about you! You're my brother! But if you're unwilling to accept even the tiniest criticism then I have no place here! I have tried with you! I really have! I love you, Ronald! But it's not I who is judging you — it's the other way around! And I can no longer take the sideways glances and constant hostility! Ever since we were children you've felt yourself superior to me! Well, this is it! I have had it! Good-bye Ronald!

RONALD. Good-bye Sydney! *(She starts to storm out — but turns around at the last second.)*

SYDNEY. Shit. I almost forgot.

RONALD. *(Irritated.)* What?

SYDNEY. I've killed Ethan. *(Their light goes out. The light comes up on Sydney's apartment, where Ethan is talking to the lump in the bed.")*

ETHAN. Sydney, it's your life. Fine. Do what you want. Stay in bed all day. If that's how you want to live your life, I can't stop you! But it would do you some good, it would do you a world of good to get out of that bed, out of this house. It would do you a lot of good to see yourself as part of something bigger, better, something more important than you. You, you, you, you, you! Not every-thing is about you. The earth's pull doesn't emanate from you, nor does the change of seasons, nor the ebb of tides. You're one person, Sydney! A crumb, a speck, a molecule, a *mark* on a molecule that means nothing. But do you ever put yourself out for the greater good? No. When I asked you to come to protest police brutality, did you? No, you turned up your nose. You snubbed the homeless and cancer research and AIDS funding and immigration, and the

27

taxi drivers and free needles and the dolphins and animal testing and school funding and day-care centers and American Indians and gay rights, and black rights and women's rights and Spanish rights and Swedish rights and Chinese rights and handicapped rights and Armenia and Bosnia and arms for hostages and Mothers Against Drunk Driving. You snubbed welfare cutbacks and arts cutbacks and housing cutbacks and school cutbacks and — *(His light goes out. The light returns to Ronald and Sydney.)*

RONALD. What?

SYDNEY. I did.

RONALD. What?

SYDNEY. I did.

RONALD. What?

SYDNEY. I did. *(Their light goes out. The light returns to Ethan, talking to the lump.)*

ETHAN. — lunch cutbacks and Medicare and Medicaid and needle exchange and government free cheese! And when Gustavo needed a bone marrow transplant, were you interested? You were not. Because it wasn't about you. You chose instead to lie there. That's right, lie there. Inert. Wallowing in the juices of your bourgeois squalor. Lie there like a corpse, like a beached sea creature, like a walrus — like the walruses you refused to help by protesting their poaching and slaughter for ivory tusks. What's wrong with you, Sydney? What is wrong with you? *(He pokes the lump. Nothing.)* Sydney? Sydney! *(He notices the gun on the floor. He picks it up.)* Oh my God. Oh Jesus. Oh Jesus. *(Light returns to Ronald and Sydney. Both apartments are lit.)*

RONALD. Sydney —

SYDNEY. What?

RONALD. Why!?

SYDNEY. You'll yell at me.

RONALD. You killed someone! I might!

SIDNEY. OK. OK. But don't tell Mom.

ETHAN. Oh my God. Oh Jesus. Sydney! Oh my God! *(He looks around in panic and drops the gun. His light goes out, leaving the light on Sydney and Ronald.)*

RONALD. Why would you do such an insane thing!?

SYDNEY. Well, I'll try to tell you the way it happened. I didn't mean to kill him!

RONALD. How'd you do it?

SYDNEY. I shot him.

RONALD. You shot him!?

SYDNEY. Three times.

RONALD. And you didn't mean to?

SYDNEY. I mean I didn't plan it. You don't know what goes on in that house. You have no idea —

RONALD. I was there last night!

SYDNEY. But you always leave early. You never stay past one. After one, boy, after one, that's when the trouble begins. Gustavo and Anthony, Cybil and Audrey, Ethan, all of them, drinking and shouting and behaving like pigs. There are pizza stains all over the rug in the living room! That's an antique rug! That's a one-of-a-kind! I hunted high and low for that rug!

RONALD. You did not.

SYDNEY. Well, the decorator did. And Philippe is the whiniest thing you ever laid eyes on! Did I ever hear it about that rug! And now ... ruined. Completely ruined —

RONALD. Get to the point!

SYDNEY. Well last night Ethan and Cybil got into a horrible argument, a hideous, unwinnable round-robin over who's suffered more, black lesbians or hispanic gays! I mean what is the point of that anyway!

RONALD. Black lesbians.

SYDNEY. Hispanic gays.

RONALD. Black lesbians.

SYDNEY. You don't know.

RONALD. What happened!?

SYDNEY. Well the shouting went on for hours! Anthony sides with Ethan, Gustavo with Cybil. Audrey and Bruno were wrestling, Greco-Roman, in the foyer, which while leaving blood stains, at least was quiet. I mean this was a row! I couldn't take it! My nerves have been on edge to begin with lately. Montana Beach has memory loss and Brick, her second husband, has some testicular disorder. And things have been very ugly between Ethan and me. I blame you, by the way —

RONALD. Me!!?

SYDNEY. If you'd never introduced us, I would never've killed him. This is all your fault!

RONALD. GET OUT! *(Their light goes out. A light comes up on Cybil, looking through her Filofax. She pauses to address the audience.)*

CYBIL. I grew up in this gigantic, green house in Larchmont. My mother liked green and my father worked for Playtex where he designed bras, to mold tits, to attract men, to imprison women. What an asshole. *(Her light goes out. The light returns to Sydney and Ronald.)*

SYDNEY. No, no, no! You've got to help me! I apologize! Here's what happened. Where was I?

RONALD. Who knows?

SYDNEY. Last night! Yes. I couldn't sleep. I need my sleep! You've seen the show, admit it! I look old, don't I? I look old! I look thirty!

RONALD. You're thirty-four!

SYDNEY. SOMEONE COULD HEAR YOU!

RONALD. Nobody cares.

SYDNEY. I couldn't sleep. I took a pill.

RONALD. One?

SYDNEY. Yes.

RONALD. Good.

SYDNEY. But I still couldn't sleep — I mean they were screaming like savages. So I took another pill.

RONALD. Two.

SYDNEY. *(Embarrassed.)* And a couple more.

RONALD. You should be a groggy, zonked-out, slack-jawed zombie!

SYDNEY. *(Sunny.)* Oh, no. I feel refreshed! I feel sunny and bright and ready for the day! *(He shakes his head in amazement as a light comes up on Cybil, talking on the phone.)*

CYBIL. Gustavo, this rally today, what's it for? ... NEITHER CAN I! *(Cybil's light goes out.)*

SYDNEY. The point is, I was pretty out of it last night. I have no idea what time Ethan came to bed. Frankly, I was surprised he came to bed at all. He comes to bed less and less often. To *my* bed, that is. God knows he's made a tour of the beds and boudoirs of *all* of our friends, all of our neighbors and, my God, even my co-workers! Why?! Why does he do this? I've done everything for that

man! I let him use my home. I let him use my car. I let him use
my credit cards! Thousands and thousands of dollars every month
for I have no idea what! What more can I do? — I never deny him
sexually. I don't know where I failed! What's wrong with me?!
RONALD. You babble! That's what's wrong with you! You babble!
SYDNEY. You're so critical. You've always been so critical. Fine,
last night at some hour, everyone left. I was asleep, thankfully, but
I assume everyone left. And Ethan crawled into my bed, stinking
like a Bowery Bum — but you know, frankly, I like that smell, on
him, mixed with sweat and this ninety-dollar-an-ounce cologne I
bought him. It's sexy. And I've been so lonely. I ran my hand over
his shoulders. He has massive shoulders — you can't tell to look at
him in clothes, but his shoulders are huge and well-muscled and
my god I'm never going to hold him again! Anyway, I ran my hand
over his shoulders and kissed the back of his neck. Normally, when
he's present, this is a signal. And, at least in the beginning, he
responded by making athletic, rhythmic and unforgettable love.
But last night, he did not!
RONALD. So, naturally, you shot him.
SYDNEY. No. No, that's not why. I'm not insane. I was kissing
the back of his head, using my tongue to play with the tiny hairs
and trace hearts in the nape of his neck. He ignored me. He
pushed me away and he mumbled indecipherably, but it couldn't
have been very loving, considering the force, the violence of the
gesture. Something in Ethan snapped last night, something very
primal snapped. He has hurt me in every way imaginable, but he's
never been violent! Until last night! And as he pushed me away he
muttered someone's name. I couldn't make it out but *it wasn't
mine*, of that much I'm sure. Tears filled my eyes but I was not to
be refused! I have poured myself into this man, and I am not to be
shunted aside. I licked his ears and stroked his hard-as-marble but-
tocks, murmuring endearments, purring I love you's, until, all at
once, with a growl, he turned over, spun over, holding his pillow
and pressed it over my face! I couldn't protest — I couldn't
breathe. I grabbed his wrists, but he had the strength of ten men!
I tugged at his arms, but they're like steel! I squirmed! I writhed! I
shrieked silently under the down ... until my eyes closed and I,
thank God, lost consciousness ... He tried to kill me, Ronald.

Ethan tried to kill me ... And so I shot him.

RONALD. *(Still.)* Oh my God.

SYDNEY. *(Weeping.)* I shot him.

RONALD. Well, then, it was self defense.

SYDNEY. Not exactly.

RONALD. He was trying to kill you.

SYDNEY. *(Matter-of-fact.)* I shot him some time later.

RONALD. Oh.

SYDNEY. I'm scared.

RONALD. We'll do something.

SYDNEY. What's going to happen to me?

RONALD. I'll think of something.

SYDNEY. *(Hysterical.)* And what's going to happen to Montana Beach! *(She collapses, in tears, into his arms. Their light goes out. Cybil's returns. She is still on the phone.)*

CYBIL. Seven! Seven! I only know, I mean really know, personally know, have as what I consider close friends, seven black people! Gustavo, I have to meet some black people! I'm serious! I need more black people, and I don't mean those white-black people, I mean black-black people. Y'know — baggy pants, gold teeth, down-trodden black people! ... I know how this happened. I do. It's Audrey. Yes! I mean she talks a good game. She marches and donates, but push come to shove, I don't think she really likes black people! I'm serious! I think, deep down she's a bigot! ... Well, yes I know *you* love her, but that's because you don't have to live with her. The constant brawling! So possessive, downright evil! You saw how she broke that guy's arm last week, when she caught us making out in the bathroom ... How dare you! How dare you say a thing like that to me! That is so typical of limited masculine thinking! MEN ARE SUCH LOSERS! Jesus Christ! Of course I'm sure I'm a lesbian! I'm a lesbian! ... BECAUSE, GOD-DAMNIT I SAY I'M A LESBIAN! I JUST HATE AUDREY! *(Cybil slams the phone down and her light goes out. The light on Ronald and Sydney returns. Sydney is still weeping.)*

SYDNEY. I hate my life. My life is over.

RONALD. Don't say that.

SYDNEY. Why not? It's true. What am I? I'm a twenty-nine-year-old soap opera actress. Even if I get off, if I claim temporary insanity —

RONALD. Temporary?

SYDNEY. Screw you. Even if I claim self-defense, or a chemical imbalance, the latter of which I think is highly likely. You know I'm on Atkins —

RONALD. What?

SYDNEY. Atkins. The Atkins diet, the all-the-protein-and-fat-you-can-shove-down-your-greasy-throat-diet. That could make a person crazy, couldn't it?

RONALD. Something has.

SYDNEY. There was that woman, that matronly woman, she shot her diet doctor and she got off!

RONALD. No she didn't.

SYDNEY. I detest you. Couldn't you let me be falsely optimistic for even a moment? So, all right, all right, I claim self-defense. Then what? The show'll drop me like a bad habit. They're just looking for some reason to get rid of me. I can tell. They think I'm fat and old. My God, they dress me in nun's outfits! At twenty-nine, I'm too old for TV and too young for prison. I can't go to prison, they'd eat me alive!

RONALD. You won't go to prison.

SYDNEY. It's all lesbians. You know that, don't you? All lesbians! They'll go insane. When, I ask you, when, do you think they've ever seen a waistline like mine! I'm scared! I don't like lesbians. I'm afraid of them.

RONALD. You like Cybil and Audrey.

SYDNEY. Not really.

RONALD. I've always known you were shallow, but I never thought you were homophobic.

SYDNEY. I'm not! I'm just scared of lesbians.

RONALD. What do you think the word means?

SYDNEY. Don't criticize me! Can't you see I'm in trouble! I have nowhere else to turn. You're my brother, you're supposed to love me! LOVE ME GODDAMN YOU! HELP ME!

RONALD. OK, OK ... stop crying. *(He hugs her.)*

SYDNEY. Thank you.

RONALD. I'll help you.

SYDNEY. You will?

RONALD. Of course.

SYDNEY. I do love you.

RONALD. I know.

SYDNEY. You're my brother.

RONALD. Are you hungry?

SYDNEY. No, no, I'm in ketosis.

RONALD. What?

SYDNEY. Deprived of carbohydrates, my body's burning fat cells for fuel.

RONALD. Oh. Well, calm down.

SYDNEY. I knew, Ronald, I knew that despite all of our differences, that you'd come through for me. — Maybe we could make it look like a suicide? Ethan drank too much and he got depressed a lot. I could forge a note, you wipe off the gun —

RONALD. Sydney?

SYDNEY. What?

RONALD. Three times. You shot him three times.

SYDNEY. Oh yes. Right. Probably hard to make that look like suicide.

RONALD. Why don't you go wash your face.

SYDNEY. That's good. That's a good idea. I'll feel better after I wash my face. *(She walks toward the bathroom and looks in.)* When did you last launder these towels?

RONALD. *(Thinking.)* Uuuuuhhhhh —

SYDNEY. I'll use toilet paper. *(She shuts the door. There is a knock at the door. Ronald opens it, revealing Ethan.)*

ETHAN. *(Frenzied.)* Someone's killed Sydney!

RONALD. ETHAN!!???

SYDNEY. *(Opening the bathroom door.)* ETHAN!!??

ETHAN. SYDNEY!!??

SYDNEY. I SHOT YOU!!

ETHAN. YOU'RE DEAD!! *(Ethan and Sydney faint.)*

RONALD. Jesus. *(The light in Ronald's apartment goes out. The light in Cybil's comes up. She is sitting on the bed, writing a note.)*

CYBIL. Dear Audrey, After much soul-searching and internal struggle I have reached the conclusion that you and I are no longer compatible. I would tell you this to your face, your gentle, loving, sweet face, but, frankly, I'm scared shitless of you. When I look back over the carnage, the mountain of injured and crippled bod-

ies you've left in your wake, I know all too well the kind of violence of which you're capable. (By the way, can you remember the name of the man you blinded in Tijuana? I can't think of it for the life of me and it's driving me crazy!) ... Shit. *(She balls up the letter and throws it on the floor. Her light goes out. Light returns to Sydney, Ronald and Ethan. Ronald rushes to help Sydney to her feet.)*
RONALD. Are you OK?
SYDNEY. It's the diet! My body's gone mad. I'm having visions! I hallucinated that Ethan was standing in your doorway!
ETHAN. *(Sitting up, coming to.)* Where am I?
SYDNEY. There it is again! *(She faints again.)*
ETHAN. Sydney?
RONALD. *(Rousing her.)* Sydney, get up!
SYDNEY. *(To Ronald.)* Oh God, Ronald! I need starch! Get me a cracker! A pretzel! A slice of bread!
RONALD. You're not hallucinating! He's here. It's Ethan! He's right here!
ETHAN. Sydney! My God, you're alive!
SYDNEY. Ethan, *you're* alive!
RONALD. *(Polite.)* You're both alive. Now leave my home. *(Sydney and Ethan embrace.)*
SYDNEY. I can't believe it! Let me feel you! Let me touch you!
ETHAN. Feel me, touch me. Go ahead.
SYDNEY. I'm so sorry, Ethan! I love you! You know I adore you! I do! I'm so very, very sorry!
ETHAN. For what?
SYDNEY. Well, shooting you for one thing — is this man generous? Is this man the most forgiving soul on the planet today, or what!?
ETHAN. I don't know what you're talking about. Do you know what she's talking about?
RONALD. Vaguely.
ETHAN. But I don't care. I'm just glad you're alive! Can I use your car? *(Ethan and Sydney kiss passionately, groping each other for a long moment.)*
RONALD. Well, this is a touching reunion.
SYDNEY. I'm sorry for all those horrible things I said to you this morning. Really! I didn't mean them!

ETHAN. I didn't hear them.

SYDNEY. And then when I thought I'd killed you, my first thought, I swear to God, my *only* thought was, how will I live, how will I survive without Ethan, my beloved Ethan!

ETHAN. Really?

SYDNEY. Ask Ronald.

RONALD. More or less.

SYDNEY. Your presumed death made me reevaluate everything. My life isn't what it should be. I'm rich and young and beautiful yet somehow unfulfilled. I think you and I should have a baby.

ETHAN. You want to have my child?

SYDNEY. *(Correcting him.)* I want to *adopt* a child. I have to think about the show. I have to think about my figure. — But that's what's missing, I think. This morning when I thought I'd shot you, everything snapped into focus. The trauma made me realize what you mean to me.

ETHAN. And when I thought *you* were dead, my first thought was ... well, similar.

SYDNEY. What?

ETHAN *(Simply repeating.)* When I thought you were —

SYDNEY. Why'd you think I was dead?

ETHAN. There's a body in your bed and a gun on the floor.

SYDNEY. The gun is mine. The body — when were you there?

ETHAN. Just now. I came straight here from there.

SYDNEY. So, what you're saying is —

ETHAN. There's a dead body, under the covers, in your bed, in your apartment.

SYDNEY. Let me understand this.

ETHAN. There's a corpse in your home.

SYDNEY. What you're telling me is —

RONALD. YOU SHOT SOMEONE ELSE!

SYDNEY. Well, that's one possibility.

RONALD. It's the only possibility!

SYDNEY. True.

ETHAN. Jesus Christ, Sydney. What have you done?

SYDNEY. Well, I thought he was you.

ETHAN. That's no excuse.

SYDNEY. He tried to suffocate me!

ETHAN. Then it's self-defense!

SYDNEY and RONALD. It's not.

ETHAN. You mean you couldn't tell the difference between me and some stranger?

SYDNEY. I'd taken some pills. I was out of it. — Where were you last night anyway?

ETHAN. Don't start in on that!

SYDNEY. I asked a simple question.

ETHAN. *(To Ronald.)* She treats me like she owns me.

SYDNEY. *(To Ronald.)* He sleeps with everyone and laughs at me behind my back.

ETHAN. Not true!

SYDNEY. True!

ETHAN. You have no business questioning me!

SYDNEY. Of course I do.

ETHAN. I was clear at the outset I'm not ready for — I am not interested in a real commitment!

SYDNEY. Oh, words! Those are just words! You vomit up words with no meaning. You say you don't want a commitment, then you move in *lock, stock and barrel!* How'm I supposed to interpret that?

ETHAN. I brought a razor blade and some underwear!

SYDNEY. You don't own anything else!

ETHAN. You said you understood! When I got evicted you said, "Live here, stay here. It's fine," you said. "We're friends," you said.

SYDNEY. We were sleeping together!

ETHAN. So?

SYDNEY. You're not stupid!

ETHAN. Oh no!?

SYDNEY. You should certainly have seen through all that "We're friends" nonsense! You moved in with me because you wanted to be more than friends! People don't sleep with their friends, Ethan! People don't screw their friends, night after night, murmuring love words, in every position, in a sweaty, savage exploration of carnal acrobatics!

ETHAN. *I* do!

SYDNEY. Well, that's just nuts.

ETHAN. I am who I am, Cookie, and I have no intention of changing. This is it. This is me. I chose to live my life entrapped by something *other* than the petty, middle-class, mind-numbing values, to which you're such a slave! I live for the big picture! Read Kerouac. Read Ginsberg.

SYDNEY. You only read the Cliff Notes!

ETHAN. Sex is a natural thing, a natural expression of friendship! The only difference between shaking hands and fucking is that I don't mind shaking hands with another man. If you want me in your life, you gotta take all of me! The good and the bad! 'Cause sometimes I'm bad! Sometimes I'm very, very bad.

SYDNEY. All right, all right! *(Ethan and Sydney embrace, kissing passionately and groping each other again.)*

RONALD. HAVE YOU FORGOTTEN THAT YOU KILLED SOMEONE!? *(Sydney and Ethan continue, sticking their heads out of their embrace to speak.)*

SYDNEY. I wonder who.

RONALD. So do I!

ETHAN. No idea.

SYDNEY. Ronald, would you go find out who it is?

RONALD. Me!?

SYDNEY. Ethan and I need some private time. We obviously have issues to work out and a relationship that merits the attention.

RONALD. No! No I will not!

SYDNEY. *(Breaking the embrace.)* Oh, c'mon. I'd do it for you.

RONALD. You would not.

SYDNEY. I might.

RONALD. Besides, I can't. I have to wait for Lance to get back.

ETHAN. Lance?

SYDNEY. Hustler.

RONALD. Boyfriend.

SYDNEY. Oh, grow up. He's not coming back. He's been gone for ages.

RONALD. Of course he is!

SYDNEY. You live in a dream world.

RONALD. You don't understand true love. You only understand manipulation.

SYDNEY. You said you'd help me!

RONALD. You have Ethan now. He can help you.

SYDNEY. *(At the door.)* Oh fine, fine! If that's your attitude.

C'mon, Ethan. *(To Ronald.)* Stay here and don't tell anyone, not a living soul, *no one,* what's going on! All right?

RONALD. Yes!

SYDNEY. Promise.

RONALD. OK!

SYDNEY. Promise!

RONALD. I promise!

SYDNEY. Thank you.

ETHAN. Do you have car keys?

SYDNEY. Will you be careful this time?

ETHAN. Don't start.

SYDNEY. You always scratch the interior. That's not Naugahyde, Mister. That's real leather! *(Sydney and Ethan leave. Ronald's light goes out, Cybil's returns. She is attempting another note.)*

CYBIL. Dear Audrey, By the time you read this, I'll be gone. As I look around the room, trying to decide what to take, trying to figure out what's mine and what's yours I'm so confused. I can't remember who stole what. I know you stole the bed, but I think I stole the mattress. I know you stole the pot, but I think I stole the wrapping papers. I wish I'd kept a journal. Looking back, I can't say there weren't good times. There were. A few. Very few. I'll never forget the day we met. We were protesting censorship, I think. At that theater. I can't remember the name of the theater or the name of the play, or why we were there. Oh wait! I remember some theater was knuckling under to the religious right. That's it. But we protested and they did the play after all. You were so courageous, hurling epithets and rocks. And when we found out they were doing the play, you asked me to come. I don't remember what it was about, or who was in it, just that it was absolutely *unwatchable.* Another victory for the left! *(She considers this, then crumples up the letter and throws it on the floor. Her light goes out. The light returns on Ronald's apartment. There is a knock at the door. He opens it, revealing Lance, who holds a guava.)*

LANCE. Here.

RONALD. You're back! I knew you'd come back!

LANCE. Man, I had to go to like twenty delis.

RONALD. You're so good.

LANCE. And I picked up a trick on my way home.

RONALD. La-ance.

LANCE. *(Proud.)* Twenty-five bucks for a hand job. — I bought some weed.

RONALD. While I appreciate your entrepreneurial enterprise, you're going to have to learn new patterns of behavior. Do you understand? You don't need to do that anymore. I'm taking care of you now.

LANCE. What do you make?

RONALD. A social worker's salary.

LANCE. Fuck that shit, man.

RONALD. We'll live on love.

LANCE. Where'd she go?

RONALD. Who?

LANCE. Guava girl.

RONALD. *(After a moment of internal debate.)* Out. Shopping. To the bank! The beauty parlor! Don't ask me!!

LANCE. Cool man, it's cool.

RONALD. I knew you'd come back! I believe in you. Let's make love.

LANCE. I thought we were going out?

RONALD. We will. Let's make love.

LANCE. I thought we were going to the park?

RONALD. We will. Let's make love.

LANCE. I thought we were going to some rally?

RONALD. We are. Let's make love. *(Their light goes out. A light comes up on Sydney's apartment. Ethan is entering. Sydney is standing in the doorway.)*

ETHAN. It's perfectly safe.

SYDNEY. You look. I'll wait in the hallway. I'll go back to Ronald's. I'll leave the country. Call me and tell me all about it.

ETHAN. Get in here.

SYDNEY. I'm scared.

ETHAN. Of what? He's already dead.

SYDNEY. What if it's someone I liked? *(Their light goes out. The light returns to Ronald and Lance.)*

RONALD. Don't you want to make love to me?

LANCE. S'not that, man.

RONALD. Don't you care for me?

40

LANCE. S'not that, man.

RONALD. Don't you find me attractive?

LANCE. S'not that, man.

RONALD. What is it?!

LANCE. You haven't paid me and the hour must be up.

RONALD. I'll write a check. *(Their light goes out. The light returns to Sydney and Ethan as she approaches the bed.)*

SYDNEY. I can't look.

ETHAN. I'll look. Just stand over there. *(He points across the room, where she goes and waits.)*

ETHAN. Here goes. *(He lifts up the blanket and is shocked by what he sees.)* Oh my God!!

SYDNEY. What, what, what? Who is it!?

ETHAN. It's Audrey!! *(The light comes up on Cybil, who is still writing a letter.)*

CYBIL. Dear Audrey, You miserable, maggot-ridden, tyrant … *(She crumples up that attempt and her light goes out.)*

SYDNEY. AUDREY!

ETHAN. Swear to God.

SYDNEY. It can't be!

ETHAN. It is! Look for yourself. *(She sort of tries to but can't.)*

SYDNEY. How can that be? I don't remember everything, but I remember enough! I remember those incredibly well-muscled, masculine broad shoulders in the night.

ETHAN. That's Audrey.

SYDNEY. I remember the hairy legs and hairy arms and hairy back!

ETHAN. That's Audrey.

SYDNEY. The smell of sweat and beer and men's cologne!

ETHAN. Audrey! All of that is Audrey! You killed Audrey! *(He lowers the blanket.)*

SYDNEY. … Oh my God. Poor, sweet, kind, gentle Audrey.

ETHAN. You said she tried to kill you.

SYDNEY. She was drunk. Nobody's perfect.

ETHAN. Now she's gone.

SYDNEY. You know what this means, don't you?

ETHAN. You were stoned and she was drunk and now you've snuffed out the life of an innocent human being?

41

SYDNEY. Well yes, that. And, that I was in bed with, stroking and touching and licking and nuzzling a woman. I came this close, this close to being a lesbian.

ETHAN. That's sort of hot.

SYDNEY. Ick.

ETHAN. What are you going to do?

SYDNEY. I don't know. I don't know, Ethan. I'm scared.

ETHAN. I'm here.

SYDNEY. Hold me. *(He takes her in his arms.)*

ETHAN. Ethan's here.

SYDNEY. I feel so safe in your arms.

ETHAN. I'll protect you.

SYDNEY. You will, won't you.

ETHAN. Bet your ass.

SYDNEY. Never let me go.

ETHAN. Shut up. *(He kisses her full on the mouth.)*

SYDNEY. Ethan! *(They sink down, behind the bed, out of sight, making love. The light comes up on Ronald and Lance as Ronald writes a check. Lance is taking off his pants, revealing boxers.)*

RONALD. If I add an extra fifty, do you think you could tell me that you love me?

LANCE. Yeah, sure, whatever.

RONALD. Thanks. *(Ronald hands Lance the check. Lance puts it in his underpants then dives into bed. As Ronald removes his pants, revealing boxer shorts, we see Ethan's hand emerge from behind Sydney's bed. It's holding her pink trousers, which he hurls away, hopefully out of a window.)*

SYDNEY. *(Head popping up.)* Be careful with those!

ETHAN. *(Head popping up.)* Shut up woman. *(Ethan kisses her and they disappear behind the bed again. By now, Ronald should have his pants off and he dives into bed with Lance. The boys disappear under the covers. These scenes remain as the light returns on Cybil.)*

CYBIL. Dear Audrey, I'm leaving. Anything I once felt for you is dead. The fact of the matter is, I stopped feeling anything a long time ago, and, if I were honest I'd have to admit, that I've stayed out of fear. I've stayed, even though I love someone else — and I do, by the way! I am capable! — I've stayed because I didn't want to admit failure. Because I feel safe and I don't want to be alone

and since I know the person I love doesn't love me, I figured you were better than nothing. But you're not. You're worse than nothing. I guess, on some level, I goaded you on. I slept around because I resented you, because you weren't who I wanted. So I tortured you and you tortured me. *(As Cybil thinks what to say next, Sydney's head pops up from behind her bed, writhing rhythmically.)*
SYDNEY. I love you, Ethan! I love you! Marry me!
ETHAN. *(Unseen.)* WHAT!?
SYDNEY. Marry me! I know it's stupid! I know it's just a piece of paper! I know it doesn't mean any — ahhhhh! *(Ethan's hand pulls Sydney out of view again.)*
CYBIL. I should have known I couldn't take it years ago. Remember when we bought that puppy? That little white puppy, Nanuk? I loved that puppy. But he peed on your books. He ruined your Sontag and your Didion. He crapped on Gertrude Stein. You made me give Nanuk away. I pleaded, I begged, but you got me in a figure-four leg lock and I acquiesced. *(Cybil thinks for a moment. Lance's head pops out from under the blanket.)*
LANCE. *(Flat, completely bored.)* That's it, man ... ooo ... yeah ... you're the greatest ... Daddy, Daddy ooo yeah. *(Something hurts him under the covers.)* OUCH!! — All right, I love you. *(Again.)* OUCH! — I love you! *(Again.)* OUCH! I said it, man! I said it! *(Lance disappears under the covers.)*
CYBIL. You have turned my life into a living hell. *(Cybil thinks a moment. Ethan's head emerges from behind the bed, his back arched, as he writhes rhythmically.)*
ETHAN. No one owns me, baby! I'm my own man! A million women tried and a million women failed! ... Oh God! *(Ronald's head pops up, out from under the blanket. He shudders in rhythmic ecstasy.)*
RONALD. Oh Jesus! Don't stop! I'll pay extra!
ETHAN. Oh God!
RONALD. Oh God!
ETHAN. Oh God!
RONALD. Oh God!
ETHAN and RONALD. OH GOD!
ETHAN, RONALD and CYBIL. *(She is still writing.)* OH GOD!!!!!! *(The lights on Sydney's apartment and Ronald's apartment go out quite abruptly, leaving Cybil to finish her thought.)*

43

CYBIL. If I WANTED TORTURE AND ABUSE I'D BE WITH A MAN! Because that's what it comes down to, Audrey! I want to be free. Free of you and free to pursue my true love! So this is it. After all the good times and bad times, the bruises and broken bones, I find I hate you! It's true. I hate you. I hate you hate you hate you hate you!! ... Love, Cybil. *(She tears the letter off the pad and leaves it on the pillow. Her light goes out. Light comes up on both Sydney and Ronald's apartments. All at once, Sydney and Ethan's heads emerge from behind the bed and Ronald and Lance emerge from under the blanket. Simultaneously, Ethan, Sydney and Ronald light a cigarette. The three of them inhale once and Lance coughs. Their lights go out. Light returns to Cybil's apartment. She pulls a suitcase out from under her bed and starts throwing random junk into it. The phone rings. She picks it up.)*
CYBIL. *(Into phone.)* Hello? ... Gustavo, yes I accept your apology, because you made me think. You made me realize that it's over, my life with Audrey is a sham and it's over ... she's not here, no ... Well, I said I'd wait for Ethan to pick me up. Yes, we'll still pick you up ... You did, you remembered!? Thank god! ... No, no, no! Chinese human rights was last month. *(Her light goes out. Light comes up on Sydney's apartment as Ethan and Sydney crawl out from behind the bed, slightly spent. He's pulling on his jeans. She's now pantless, but her jacket should be plenty long. Her costume should look like a hot-pink version of Judy Garland's tuxedo jacket and tights.)*
SYDNEY. That was amazing. You are unbelievable.
ETHAN. Thanks, babe.
SYDNEY. The power! The force! The pent-up energy. It felt like I was the first woman you'd been with in years.
ETHAN. *(As if it were longer.)* Hours.
SYDNEY. *(Sits up, suddenly disturbed.)* Ethan. Do you think I took in carbohydrates?
ETHAN. What?
SYDNEY. I'm on Atkins. I'm not allowed carbohydrates. You don't think —
ETHAN. I don't think.
SYDNEY. Thank God. *(Their light goes out. The light comes up on Ronald and Lance in bed, putting on their pants.)*
LANCE. Bite me like that again, man, and I'll cut your ass.

RONALD. I'm sorry. I just got carried away. I got swept up in a frenzy of passion, a vortex of lust —

LANCE. OK, OK, OK.

RONALD. Let's talk about our future.

LANCE. Whatever.

RONALD. What do you want to do with your life?

LANCE. I dunno.

RONALD. There must be something, some secret ambition you've always harbored. When you shut your eyes what do you see yourself doing?

LANCE. I dunno.

RONALD. Where would you like to be in ten years?

LANCE. I'd like to be really, really ... high. *(Their light goes out. Light returns to Sydney and Ethan. They are still on the floor, spent.)*

SYDNEY. I think we should get married.

ETHAN. What?

SYDNEY. Think. You and I. Mr. and Mrs. Ethan Swallow.

ETHAN. Why?

SYDNEY. I think I'd be much more able to tolerate your constant philandering if we were married.

ETHAN. No.

SYDNEY. Why not?

ETHAN. I don't want to.

SYDNEY. Is it me? Is it that you don't want to marry me? Do you not want to get married at all, or is it me?

ETHAN. It's you.

SYDNEY. Oh. I see. Well. Then I don't think we should see each other any more.

ETHAN. All right.

SYDNEY. Don't leave me!

ETHAN. I am who I am!!

SYDNEY. *(Disturbed.)* You've based all of your behavioral patterns on a catchphrase from Popeye — which, by the way, I believe you're paraphrasing.

ETHAN. I couldn't marry you. We have completely different values.

SYDNEY. Well, if you're going to pick nits you'll never find someone.

ETHAN. I mean the sex is great, but, I find you ethically corrupt.

SYDNEY. That doesn't stop you from spending my money on

45

God knows what like a drunken sailor on a three-day leave.

ETHAN. I find you morally bankrupt.

SYDNEY. All right, I get it. No marriage. Fine. Then I think we should live together.

ETHAN. We already do. *(The light comes up on Cybil, still on the phone.)*

CYBIL. The rain forest was three weeks ago! *(Cybil's light goes out.)*

ETHAN. We should tell Cybil.

SYDNEY. Tell her what?

ETHAN. That Audrey's dead.

SYDNEY. Oh, yes, of course. I was still on "It's me you don't want to marry."

ETHAN. She'll be devastated. Audrey's her life, her whole life. I don't know that I've ever seen a couple more in love and devoted to each other.

SYDNEY. You tell her.

ETHAN. *You* shot her.

SYDNEY. I don't like confrontations. I'm afraid of confrontations. Cybil curses a lot.

ETHAN. You owe it to her, Sydney.

SYDNEY. I have a better idea. Let's go to a hardware store and buy a big trunk! Do you still have my credit cards?

ETHAN. Yes.

SYDNEY. We'll buy a big trunk! We'll put Audrey in it and dump it in the river! Cybil never has to know!

ETHAN. What'll that accomplish? It's bound to wash up.

SYDNEY. Then we'll buy a big trunk, stuff Audrey in it and ship it to France. I have an old boyfriend there — we hardly ever speak. Paulo was mad about me. He'll be so touched when he sees the return address.

ETHAN. One thing at a time!

SYDNEY. OK. A) We'll buy a big trunk —

ETHAN. No, no, no! First you tell Cybil!

SYDNEY. She'll yell at me!

ETHAN. I assume she will.

SYDNEY. She's never liked me. And I don't know why! I have bent over backwards to ingratiate myself to that miserable hag. I know for a fact that she's the one who broke my sixteenth-century

Ming vase in the foyer. That vase cost a fortune! But did I say anything? Did I point a finger or demand remuneration? I did not.

ETHAN. A vase is a thing. It's replaceable. A human life is not.

SYDNEY. You try to replace a sixteenth-century Ming vase.

ETHAN. We'll tell Cybil and then we'll figure out what to do with the body.

SYDNEY. *(Looking for her pants.)* I could've made a big stink about that vase, but I let it go. Now, I wish I'd said something — Where are my pants? Have you seen my pants?

ETHAN. I threw them out the window.

SYDNEY. Jesus Christ, Ethan! This is a suit and I paid retail! This isn't from some sample sale! I didn't steal it from wardrobe! Now what am I supposed to wear with this jacket?!

ETHAN. You look fine.

SYDNEY. I look like I should burst into a musical number.

ETHAN. I think it's hot.

SYDNEY. Really?

ETHAN. Uh-huh.

SYDNEY. Well, all right. But if we have to tell Cybil, let's hurry up! Let's get it over with. C'mon! God, I feel queasy. I just hope she's hungover. It's been my experience that it's much easier to forcibly subdue someone when they're very, very hungover. *(Sydney exits. Ethan addresses the audience.)*

ETHAN. I grew up in a house as big as a hospital. My father was a neurosurgeon — *(Sydney sticks her head through the door.)*

SYDNEY. Would you come on! We don't have time for that! *(Ethan nods and follows her. Their light goes out. Light comes up on Ronald and Lance. They are seated on the bed.)*

RONALD. It's important to belong to something. The need to be part of a bigger whole is basic to the human condition.

LANCE. *(Amused.)* A bigger hole. I get it.

RONALD. What I'm saying is, so many of us feel estranged from our families, at least from our birth families — are you close to yours?

LANCE. Well, man, I mean —

RONALD. That's why we create new families. Do you understand? Now *we'll* be a family. How do you feel about children?

LANCE. I never touch 'em!

RONALD. I've always wanted children. A little girl who would look up to me. Or a boy I could dress in fancy clothes.

LANCE. *(Looking around.)* Did you see my pot?

RONALD. There's nothing that makes one feel more needed than *being* needed. The gaze of hungry, begging eyes feels like love. Trust me. I think I've sublimated my parental instinct into my work. But now it's time for a real child. We should adopt a baby!

LANCE. What?

RONALD. We should! It'll be wonderful. They're letting lots of gay people adopt children these days — which *is* odd, since they won't let us teach them in public schools. But one thing at a time. And we could get a crack baby! Or a special-needs child! Like Mia Farrow! *(Lance finds his pot and lights a joint.)*

LANCE. Mia who?

RONALD. God put us here for a reason, Lance. If you believe in God. Do you believe in God?

LANCE. No.

RONALD. Neither do I.

LANCE. You want a hit?

RONALD. No thank you. Do you think you're ready for the responsibilities of fatherhood?

LANCE. No way.

RONALD. Motherhood?

LANCE. Fuck you.

RONALD. Well, maybe it is too soon. You've only known dependence. We should start smaller. A dog. Do you like dogs?

LANCE. Dogs are cool.

RONALD. Yes. We'll get a dog. A poodle or a Portuguese Water Dog. They are so cute! And he'll be your responsibility. You'll love him and walk him and groom him.

LANCE. Fuck that shit, man.

RONALD. OK, OK. No dog ... A plant! We'll start with a plant.

LANCE. Do I gotta water it?

RONALD. A cactus. We'll put it over there. Very low maintenance. We'll start with a plant, then a dog, then a baby. You'll see, you'll be happy. We should have a commitment ceremony! *(Their light goes out. Light comes up on Cybil's apartment. Sydney and Ethan are standing in the door. Cybil's holding her suitcase.)*

CYBIL. I thought you'd never get back. Let's go, let's go, let's go.
ETHAN. Sit down, Cybil.
CYBIL. No time for that! We're late. Ethan, take the firebombs.
Sydney — if you're coming, the stink bombs. Gustavo's waiting!
ETHAN. Sit down, Cybil!!
CYBIL. What is it? What's wrong.
ETHAN. Go ahead, Sydney.
SYDNEY. Cybil, do you remember that vase in my foyer? Very fancy, very old?
CYBIL. I DIDN'T TOUCH YOUR STINKIN' VASE!
SYDNEY. And that night table looks eerily like one I had *until last week.*
ETHAN. Sydney!!
SYDNEY. Sorry.
ETHAN. Go ahead.
SYDNEY. OK, here goes. Cybil. I am so embarrassed. I don't know how to say this. Just promise me, you won't yell at me —
ETHAN. SYDNEY!
SYDNEY. All right! ... *(Mumbling indecipherably:)* I killed Audrey.
CYBIL. What? What did you say? What'd she say?
SYDNEY. *(Mumbling.)* I killed Audrey.
CYBIL. Do you understand her? I didn't understand her. What did you say?
SYDNEY. I KILLED AUDREY! *(The light comes up on Lance and Ronald.)*
LANCE. A what?
RONALD. A wedding! We should have a wedding! *(The light on Lance and Ronald goes out.)*
CYBIL. *(Stunned.)* Oh ... Oh ... Oh my.
SYDNEY. There. I told her. Can we go now? I'd like to look for my pants.
ETHAN. No.
CYBIL. I can't believe it. She's gone? Audrey is gone? My Audrey is ...
SYDNEY. Gone, dead, shot, finished, adios. Can we go?
CYBIL. I can't breathe ... I can't! I can't! There's no air! *(Ethan puts his arm around her shoulder.)*
ETHAN. I can only imagine what you're going through, Cybil. I

know how devoted you two were to each other. *(Cybil crumples her "good-bye" letter up, behind her back.)*
CYBIL. Yes, it's true, we were. We loved each other. Really, deeply, truly loved each other. Did you pass the garden on your way up? Audrey and I planted those flowers the night I moved in. And we watched them grow, as our love grew, season after season.
SYDNEY. You mean that patch of dried-up dirt?
CYBIL. Yes, that's it. It was a tribute.
ETHAN. Go ahead. Lash out. Strike someone if you want to.
SYDNEY. Ethan!
CYBIL. *(Swinging and missing Sydney.)* YOU KILLED MY AUDREY!!!!!
SYDNEY. It was an accident!
CYBIL. *(Sadly.)* Oh. All right, I forgive you then.
ETHAN. She's mad with grief.
CYBIL. I am! I am! Oh miser   ll be my handmaiden now!
SYDNEY. Well, that's dement
CYBIL. I shall know only darkness and grief! From now on I wear only black!
SYDNEY. As opposed to your usual Day-Glo-Pucci pallet?
CYBIL. I shall eschew all shades of gray!
ETHAN. There, there.
CYBIL. Comfort me, Ethan. Hold me. I need to get away. This city is ruined for me. This foul city with its broken concrete and dirty alleys. Every fetid odor will remind me of Audrey! Every piece of filthy litter I see will look like her! I need to escape. Perhaps an island. Someplace tropical. — Have either of you ever been to St. Barts?
SYDNEY. I have.
CYBIL. Oh to lie on the sand and forget my tragedy. I must bake in the blazing sun, day after day, and become someone else!
SYDNEY. A Nubian?
ETHAN. You should. You should get away.
CYBIL. How can I? I have nothing?! I couldn't get as far the Newark airport on my savings. I'm a prisoner in this dungeon of torment!
ETHAN. Sydney will pay for it.
SYDNEY. WHAT?!

CYBIL. Would you?! Would you really do that for me?

SYDNEY. No.

ETHAN. Sydney, you shot her true love. It's the least you can do.

SYDNEY. St. Barts is ridiculously overpriced. A week in Miami or bubkis.

CYBIL. Oh thank you! Thank you so much! You're an angel, sort of. I know I'll be able to put this behind me someday, after years of losing myself in foreign cities. I've never seen Europe, you know.

ETHAN. You'll see, Sydney, purging yourself of money will cleanse you.

SYDNEY. Then leave me dirty.

CYBIL. I'll need some beachwear. A caftan, maybe. Or a sarong. Can Ethan come with me? Can he, can he, can he?

SYDNEY. Cybil?

CYBIL. What?

SYDNEY. Why were you packing?

CYBIL. Packing?

SYDNEY. This suitcase — why were you packing?

CYBIL. I don't remember. Everything is blurry. My life is lived in two volumes. Before Audrey and after. I remember so little of my frivolous past. *(Sydney picks up one of the discarded letters.)*

SYDNEY. And what's this?

CYBIL. I'm writing a novel?

SYDNEY. You were leaving Audrey, weren't you?

CYBIL. No. We were very happy.

SYDNEY. *(Satisfied, tossing it.)* Oh, OK. It looked like a good-bye letter.

CYBIL. ALL RIGHT I WAS! FINE! FINE! I HATED HER GUTS! YOU TORTURED IT OUT OF ME! *(Their light goes out. Light comes up on Ronald and Lance. Ronald is sitting with a pad and paper.)*

RONALD. The key to an exciting party is the theme. I've always liked tropical themes. You know, like Krakatoa East of Java or a luau theme.

LANCE. Cool.

RONALD. Then you do up the room in bright colors. It's festive! And you hang coconuts, put place cards in seashells. And poi, poi,

51

poi flowing freely!

LANCE. Cool.

RONALD. We can serve coconut cream pie and lots of fish. Do you like fish?

LANCE. No.

RONALD. OK. Ix-nay on the ish-fay. How about chicken?

LANCE. Chicken's cool.

RONALD. It's not very tropical, but that's OK. It serves no one to be rigid. This is going to be so much fun! Are you excited!?

LANCE. *(Realizing it.)* Yeah.

RONALD. Good, good, good! Now the guest list. Let's see. I'll have to have Sydney. And Gustavo and Audrey and Cybil and Ethan and Bruno and Anthony and not my parents but everyone from my office. I'll have, let's say, thirty. I can make do with thirty. So you can have thirty. But no old tricks. I don't think that'd be appropriate. Shoot.

LANCE. Well, I should invite Scar —

RONALD. You think?

LANCE. Yeah.

RONALD. All right, all right. Who else? *(Lance thinks for a long moment.)*

LANCE. Did I say Scar?

RONALD. You did. Who else. *(Lance thinks again for a long moment. Light comes up on Cybil, Sydney and Ethan.)*

CYBIL. She was a pig. I stuck with her 'cause I was lonely! I've been so lonely! *(Cybil collapses into Ethan's arms.)*

ETHAN. It's all right, Cybil.

CYBIL. I never loved her! I've loved someone else for years. For centuries. But he doesn't know I'm alive!

SYDNEY. He?

CYBIL. Did I say he? I meant she. HOLD ME, ETHAN! *(Cybil kisses Ethan full on the mouth for a long moment. Sydney gasps in horror.)*

LANCE. Did I say Scar?

RONALD. You did. Who else. *(Ethan pushes Cybil away.)*

ETHAN. CYBIL!

CYBIL. I'm sorry! I can't help it! I LOVE YOU!

SYDNEY. I thought you were this big ol' lesbian!

CYBIL. Maybe I am, maybe I'm not what's it to you, *Missy!?*

SYDNEY. Well at the moment it seems very important!

CYBIL. Politically! I'm a lesbian politically! Isn't that enough!

SYDNEY. Not for me. No, it's not and get off of my boyfriend.

CYBIL. Tell me we have a chance, Ethan! Tell me you have feelings for me!

ETHAN. But we don't have a chance and I don't have feelings for you.

CYBIL. You sang a different tune last night!

SYDNEY. Jesus Christ Ethan!

ETHAN. Well, I thought you were hot when you were a lesbian.

CYBIL. I want to die. *(She sits on the bed and starts eating a Snickers bar.)*

LANCE. Did I say Scar?

RONALD. You did. Who else? *(The light on Ronald and Lance goes out.)*

CYBIL. I'm just going to eat and eat until I explode. I just want to be this big fat, lonely lump of crud.

SYDNEY. Well, I'm glad someone's happy. I'm going to prison unless we think of something!

ETHAN. You can't go to prison!

SYDNEY. Well, do you have a plan?

ETHAN. We'll ransack your home and make it look like a break-in!

SYDNEY. Absolutely not! That's a co-op. I own that apartment. And besides the expense, if word gets out, I'll never get board approval again!

CYBIL. I hate men! I hate women! I hate everyone!

ETHAN. Let me think. Let me think.

CYBIL. Oh let her go! Let her go to prison! Who cares! Who needs her anyway!

ETHAN. We do, Cybil! We need her! We need her house and her car and her stuff. That armoire brought three grand! And fire-bombs don't grow on trees! Leaflets don't print themselves! We need her money! We need her credit cards! How do you think I bailed out Gustavo when he got arrested!

SYDNEY. That's what that charge was!?

ETHAN. Sorry.

SYDNEY. Forget it.

ETHAN. The point is *we* need her!

SYDNEY. *(Ironic.)* I feel so loved.

ETHAN. Oh shut up, Sydney! I love you.

SYDNEY. You do?

ETHAN. Well, obviously!

SYDNEY. *(Happy.)* Good.

CYBIL. I don't want to think. I want to eat. I want to eat and eat and eat. And then I want to eat some more.

SYDNEY. *(Calmer.)* I know what to do.

ETHAN. What?

SYDNEY. It's horrible ... But I know what to do. Listen to me. *(The light goes out. Sydney steps into a pool of light.)* It came to her all at once, in one piece. She didn't even know she could have such thoughts. *(Lights come up on Ronald and Lance, who are as they were. Sydney watches them. They do not see her.)*

LANCE. I'm thinking.

RONALD. There must be someone. There must be lots of people.

LANCE. Did I say Scar?

RONALD. You did. Who else?

LANCE. I'm thinking. *(Ronald's phone rings. He picks it up.)*

RONALD. Hello?

SYDNEY. Did he come back?

RONALD. He did. I was right and you were wrong.

SYDNEY. Did you tell him anything?

RONALD. We have other concerns.

SYDNEY. Come over to Cybil's —

RONALD. I can't right now —

SYDNEY. And come alone. Drop what you're doing. Get over to Cybil's as fast as you can. *(Sydney's light goes out.)*

RONALD. *(Putting on his shoes.)* I have to go. I'm sorry. But I'll be back. While I'm gone, you can work on your list.

LANCE. OK.

RONALD. *(Sweetly.)* And you don't have to have twenty-nine. You can have as many or as few as you want.

LANCE. Cool. *(Ronald exits. Lance takes a drag on his joint, for courage, then dials the phone.)* Hey, Scar. It's me, Lance ... Yeah, I'm OK ... Well, I don't know ... tonight? No, I don't think so ... don't fuckin' yell at me, man! ... DON'T YELL AT ME, MAN!! ... I'm callin' for a reason ... I'm not comin' back ... no ... no ... I'm not

... Fuck you, man! ... No, it's not a new — it's not ... I met someone ... he's cool ... he is ... I trust him ... I'm gonna live here —
I'm gonna live here! ... I can too! Fuck you, I can! I can do any
fuckin' thing I want!! ... I don't owe you shit, man! ... Well, fuck
you then, just fuck you too!! *(He slams down the phone. A moment
passes. He goes to the bed and picks up the pad on which Ronald was
writing the guest list. He crosses out Scar. He feels defeated.)* ... Shit.
*(He sits for a moment, then his light slowly fades out. Once Lance's light
is out, light comes up on Cybil's apartment. Ronald has joined Sydney,
Ethan and Cybil. Cybil now has a one-pound bag of M&Ms.)*
RONALD. *(Stunned, still.)* No.
SYDNEY. Ronald —
RONALD. No!!
ETHAN. It's the only way out.
RONALD. I love him!!
CYBIL. Love?
ETHAN. Think about it.
CYBIL. Spare me love.
RONALD. YOU HAVE NO RIGHT!
CYBIL. Keep love —
SYDNEY. I'm your sister.
CYBIL. Gimme M&Ms.
RONALD. YOU HAVE NO RIGHT TO DO THIS!!
SYDNEY. You said you'd help me.
RONALD. YOU CAN NOT DO THIS!
CYBIL. Food. Food lasts. Love dies.
RONALD. I won't listen!
ETHAN. Ronald —
RONALD. I WON'T LISTEN TO THIS!
ETHAN. How long could it last?
RONALD. *(Near tears.)* FUCK YOU!
ETHAN. A week, a month?
SYDNEY. We're talking about my life.
CYBIL. I thought he was a junkie? Isn't he a junkie?
ETHAN. He is.
RONALD. So what!?
CYBIL. *(Eating.)* I'm just saying be honest.
SYDNEY. You've told me yourself —

CYBIL. The streets are full of them.

RONALD. NO!

CYBIL. *(Casual, dismissive.)* There are bodies everywhere.

ETHAN. Twenty-year-olds, kids.

CYBIL. Every day.

RONALD. NO!!

SYDNEY. You just met him.

CYBIL. Everywhere you look.

SYDNEY. You don't know him!

RONALD. YOU CAN'T DO THIS!

CYBIL. It's so sad.

RONALD. YOU CAN'T DO THIS TO HIM!

SYDNEY. Who knows what'll happen?

RONALD. YOU CAN'T DO IT TO ME!

SYDNEY. Something could happen.

ETHAN. Isn't this what we've always talked about?

SYDNEY. I need you.

RONALD. What do I have?

ETHAN. Putting our personal happiness *behind* the greater good?

RONALD. What do I have?!

ETHAN. Personal sacrifice?

SYDNEY. You promised.

RONALD. WHAT DO I HAVE!? ... I HAVE NOTHING! I HAVE NOTHING! FUCKING NOTHING! I HAVE HIM! DO YOU UNDERSTAND THAT!? I HAVE HIM AND I LOVE HIM! GODDAMN YOU! GODDAMN YOU TO HELL!! *(Pause.)*

ETHAN. *(Flat.)* We have to do something. We have to do this. We have no power without money. We have no money without Sydney.

RONALD. Please.

ETHAN. And we've done things. We have mattered. We've changed people ... and lives.

RONALD. ... I love him.

SYDNEY. *(Reaching for him.)* And I love you, Ronald.

ETHAN. We need her.

SYDNEY. I love you. *(A moment passes. Ronald is completely defeated. The others watch him, but get no sign of acquiescence.*

56

Finally, slowly, the lights come up on Ronald's apartment, revealing Lance seated on the bed as he was. Once the lights are up full, everyone can see everyone else, as if there were no separation between the two rooms. And when they move into Ronald's apartment, they do so directly, not through a door, but through the imaginary wall.)

LANCE. *(Cheerful, looking up.)* Hey.

SYDNEY. Lance, this is Ethan, and Cybil.

CYBIL. *(Entering Ronald's apartment.)* M&M?

LANCE. Cool. *(She gives him the bag.)* Your guava's over there. *(Sydney crosses into Ronald's apartment and picks it up.)*

ETHAN. *(Entering Ronald's apartment.)* Nice to meet you.

LANCE. Yeah.

ETHAN. Could you do us a favor?

LANCE. We goin' to the rally?

ETHAN. We are —

SYDNEY. In a bit.

LANCE. What's it for?

ETHAN. We need you to go —

CYBIL. I'm calling Gustavo. *(Cybil dials the phone.)*

SYDNEY. Here's the address.

ETHAN. Her apartment.

CYBIL. *(Into the phone.)* Gustavo?

ETHAN. There's a gun.

CYBIL. *(Into the phone.)* We're on our way.

SYDNEY. There's a key —

ETHAN. Bring it to us.

SYDNEY. Under the mat.

CYBIL. *(Into the phone.)* Wait outside.

ETHAN. Bring it to us.

SYDNEY. Our friend is waiting.

ETHAN. In the park.

CYBIL. *(Into the phone.)* I gotta hang up. *(She does so.)*

LANCE. Tompkins Square?

ETHAN. You don't mind?

LANCE. *(Shrugging.)* I don't mind.

SYDNEY. Meet us there.

LANCE. Where's Ronald?

RONALD. *(Quietly, from Cybil's apartment.)* I'm here, Lance.

CYBIL. *(Taking back the M&Ms.)* Give me those.
RONALD. I'm here, Lance.
LANCE. OK.
ETHAN. Good.
LANCE. In the park.
ETHAN. Thanks a lot. *(Ronald rushes into his apartment.)*
LANCE. *(To Ronald.)* I'll work on the list tonight. *(The others watch, or turn away, in silence, as Ronald walks to Lance and kisses him, passionately on the mouth.)*
RONALD. I love you, Lance.
LANCE. *(Under his breath, embarrassed.)* Shut up, man.
RONALD. I love you.
LANCE. C'mon!
RONALD. Sorry.
LANCE. *(Cheerful.)* See you there. *(Lance rushes out the door. There is a pall over the group.)*
SYDNEY. ... I'll make the call.
CYBIL. *(Eating.)* Then we really should go. Gustavo's pissed off.
RONALD. I'm not going.
ETHAN. You have to.
RONALD. I don't.
ETHAN. We need you.
RONALD. Too bad.
ETHAN. You can't give up. You know that. You've devoted your whole life to other people. You're the one. You're the one who told me you can never give up. There are too many of them. There are too many rocks, and the rocks are hate. And they're usually wrapped in pages from the Bible. You told me that. Remember?
RONALD. Yes.
ETHAN. Remember that.
SYDNEY. *(Into the phone.)* Hello? ... Yes ... I need to report a crime — *(Their light goes out abruptly. A light comes up on Lance, who addresses the audience.)*
LANCE. I was born in Montana. My mother worked in a five-and-ten and then a beauty parlor. My father was missing before I was born. But there was always a man in the house — until I was ten, and then I don't know. My mother's boyfriend hated kids and so she had to choose. I hit the road. *(The light comes up around him.*

He is in Sydney's apartment, standing at the bed. Slowly he picks up the gun. As he does so, we hear the sound of a siren and see the flashing red light, in the distance at first, but getting closer and closer. He stands, frozen, looks out the window. The light returns to Ronald's apartment. The group is as they were. Lance's light begins to fade out slowly.)

CYBIL. I have eaten an entire pound of M&Ms.

ETHAN. What's your point?

CYBIL. My point is we have to stop at a deli on the way.

SYDNEY. I'm sorry, Ronald.

CYBIL. Or a grocery store.

ETHAN. Fine.

CYBIL. Or an outlet of some kind. Some kind of candy outlet.

SYDNEY. I've been thinking. I don't understand. Why don't you meet people?

CYBIL. You know what I've never had? A Zagnut bar.

SYDNEY. I mean you know they say power is an aphrodisiac. Well, I can't think of anyone more powerful than a social services caseworker. You must have dozens of cute runaways and homeless orphans who rely on you for their checks. *(Lance's light fades out.)*

RONALD. I suppose.

SYDNEY. Well, use it, for God's sake.

CYBIL. *(Licking her fingers.)* It's true! When I visited you last time — there was that adorable guy waiting for an interview. He was delicious!

RONALD. Scott, I think you mean Scott.

CYBIL. Yeah. He had a killer ass. We had sex in the bathroom at your office.

RONALD. I thought you were a lesbian.

CYBIL. Don't start. I've had a bad day.

SYDNEY. You could be using your administrative power to get laid all over the place.

RONALD. Hmmm.

CYBIL. I remember!

ETHAN. What?

CYBIL. The rally! I remember what it's for!!

ETHAN, SYDNEY and RONALD. What?

CYBIL. José Santo Domingo!

ETHAN. His name's not Santo Domingo! He's FROM Santo

Domingo!
CYBIL. Don't pick on me, I'm having a sugar drop!
SYDNEY. Who's that?
ETHAN. An innocent kid —
CYBIL. A darling boy!
ETHAN. Convicted —
CYBIL. Falsely! Absolutely falsely!
ETHAN. There was NO evidence whatsoever!
RONALD. Of murder.
SYDNEY. My God!
ETHAN. He was completely railroaded. They never had a shred of evidence to link him to anything! But they gave him some lawyer, some court-appointed lawyer, a buffoon who never tried anything more than a traffic ticket! And now they're gonna execute him!
CYBIL. *(To Ronald.)* Have you seen his picture?
RONALD. I have.
CYBIL. Is he gorgeous?
RONALD. He's gorgeous.
SYDNEY. They're going to execute him?
ETHAN. Tomorrow!
CYBIL. They're fryin' his ass tomorrow!
SYDNEY. My God —
CYBIL. *(Fist in the air.)* WE'RE COMING, JOSÉ! WE'RE COMING TO SAVE YOU!
SYDNEY. A perfectly innocent kid. Terrible.
CYBIL. I can feel it already! The crowd! THE CHANTS! I knew it was stink bombs! You don't bring firebombs to an antideath penalty rally! It's counterproductive!!
ETHAN. *(At the door.)* You coming, Sydney?
SYDNEY. What the hell.
CYBIL. Capital punishment is murder!
ETHAN. State-sanctioned murder!
CYBIL. WE CAN STOP THEM! WE CAN!! IF THERE'S ENOUGH OF US! IF WE SHOUT LOUD ENOUGH AND LONG ENOUGH THEY CAN'T IGNORE US! FUCK THE CHAIR! FUCK THE D.A.! FUCK THE GOVERNOR AND THE RIGHT WING AND NUCLEAR POWER!!
SYDNEY. *(Passing Cybil.)* Nuclear power?

CYBIL. Shut up, I don't know. FUCK CITY HALL! *(Ethan passes Cybil.)* You said we could stop at a market.

ETHAN. Yes. Fine, fine, we'll stop at a market.

CYBIL. FUCK THE PIGS!!! *(Cybil exits.)*

ETHAN. Are you coming, Sydney?

SYDNEY. I don't know — it's sunny out and I tend to freckle —

ETHAN. Sydney!! *(Ethan exits. Sydney stands, looking at Ronald for a moment, then turns and exits. Ronald sighs, not sure of what to do. He decides and grabs his keys. The phone rings. He answers it.)*

RONALD. *(Into the phone.)* Yes Gustavo, we're on our way. *(He hangs up, then addresses the audience.)* You never know, there could be someone cute. *(To the gang, as he rushes out.)* Wait for me, goddamnit!! *(He shuts the door behind him. Blackout.)*

End of Play

PROPERTY LIST

Cigarette and lighter/matches
Phone
Purse (SYDNEY)
Gun (SYDNEY, ETHAN, LANCE)
T-shirt that reads "Fuck [insert name of present mayor of New
    York] (ETHAN)
Wallet (RONALD)
Take-out cup of coffee (ETHAN)
Black jeans (ETHAN, RONALD, LANCE)
Doc Martens (ETHAN, RONALD, LANCE)
Can of red spray paint (CYBIL)
A joint and lighter/matches (SYDNEY, LANCE)
Twenty dollars (SYDNEY)
Filofax (CYBIL)
Paper and writing utensil (CYBIL, RONALD)
Guava (LANCE)
Checkbook and writing utensil (RONALD)
Suitcase (CYBIL)
Random junk (CYBIL)
Snickers bar (CYBIL)
Shoes (RONALD)
Bag of M&Ms (CYBIL)
Keys (RONALD)

SOUND EFFECTS

Phone ringing
Gunshots
Siren

NEW PLAYS

★ **CLYBOURNE PARK by Bruce Norris.** WINNER OF THE 2011 PULITZER PRIZE AND 2012 TONY AWARD. Act One takes place in 1959 as community leaders try to stop the sale of a home to a black family. Act Two is set in the same house in the present day as the now predominantly African-American neighborhood battles to hold its ground. "Vital, sharp-witted and ferociously smart." *–NY Times.* "A theatrical treasure...Indisputably, uproariously funny." *–Entertainment Weekly.* [4M, 3W] ISBN: 978-0-8222-2697-0

★ **WATER BY THE SPOONFUL by Quiara Alegría Hudes.** WINNER OF THE 2012 PULITZER PRIZE. A Puerto Rican veteran is surrounded by the North Philadelphia demons he tried to escape in the service. "This is a very funny, warm, and yes uplifting play." *–Hartford Courant.* "The play is a combination poem, prayer and app on how to cope in an age of uncertainty, speed and chaos." *–Variety.* [4M, 3W] ISBN: 978-0-8222-2716-8

★ **RED by John Logan.** WINNER OF THE 2010 TONY AWARD. Mark Rothko has just landed the biggest commission in the history of modern art. But when his young assistant, Ken, gains the confidence to challenge him, Rothko faces the agonizing possibility that his crowning achievement could also become his undoing. "Intense and exciting." *–NY Times.* "Smart, eloquent entertainment." *–New Yorker.* [2M] ISBN: 978-0-8222-2483-9

★ **VENUS IN FUR by David Ives.** Thomas, a beleaguered playwright/director, is desperate to find an actress to play Vanda, the female lead in his adaptation of the classic sadomasochistic tale *Venus in Fur.* "Ninety minutes of good, kinky fun." *–NY Times.* "A fast-paced journey into one man's entrapment by a clever, vengeful female." *–Associated Press.* [1M, 1W] ISBN: 978-0-8222-2603-1

★ **OTHER DESERT CITIES by Jon Robin Baitz.** Brooke returns home to Palm Springs after a six-year absence and announces that she is about to publish a memoir dredging up a pivotal and tragic event in the family's history—a wound they don't want reopened. "Leaves you feeling both moved and gratifyingly sated." *–NY Times.* "A genuine pleasure." *–NY Post.* [2M, 3W] ISBN: 978-0-8222-2605-5

★ **TRIBES by Nina Raine.** Billy was born deaf into a hearing family and adapts brilliantly to his family's unconventional ways, but it's not until he meets Sylvia, a young woman on the brink of deafness, that he finally understands what it means to be understood. "A smart, lively play." *–NY Times.* "[A] bright and boldly provocative drama." *–Associated Press.* [3M, 2W] ISBN: 978-0-8222-2751-9

DRAMATISTS PLAY SERVICE, INC.
440 Park Avenue South, New York, NY 10016 212-683-8960 Fax 212-213-1539
postmaster@dramatists.com   www.dramatists.com